MEATBALLS FOR THE PEOPLE

proverbs to chew on

GARY SOTO
≈

 Red Hen Press | *Pasadena, CA*

Several of the proverbs appeared in *Hubbub* and *Long Dumb Voices*.

Book layout by Kimberly Daigle   OCT 2 4 2017

Library of Congress Cataloging-in-Publication Data

Names: Soto, Gary author.
Title: Meatballs for the people : proverbs to chew on / Gary Soto.
Description: First edition. | Pasadena, CA : Red Hen Press, 2017.
Identifiers: LCCN 2017011416 | ISBN 9781597096010 (pbk. : alk. paper)
Subjects: LCSH: Proverbs.
Classification: LCC PN6405 .S68 2017 | DDC 398.9—dc23
LC record available at https://lccn.loc.gov/2017011416

The National Endowment for the Arts, the Los Angeles County Arts Com-
mission, the Dwight Stuart Youth Fund, the Max Factor Family Founda-
tion, the Pasadena Tournament of Roses Foundation, the Pasadena Arts &
Culture Commission and the City of Pasadena Cultural Affairs Division,
the City of Los Angeles Department of Cultural Affairs, the Audrey & Syd-
ney Irmas Charitable Foundation, Sony Pictures Entertainment, Amazon
Literary Partnership, and the Sherwood Foundation partially support Red
Hen Press.

First Edition
Published by Red Hen Press
www.redhen.org

In memory of Jon Veinberg,
poet and phrasemaker

MEATBALLS FOR THE PEOPLE

≈

PREFACE

At the heart of a proverb is poetry, and poetry has been my art since I was a long-haired young man in the early 1970s. A sound proverb is the epitome of wisdom, as in "Haste makes waste," or "A penny saved is a penny earned." The proverb stops us for a moment—true, we think, very true. Pennies add up to dollars; shoelaces tied in a hurry soon demand our attention. Proverbs, then, might be cautionary tales without the tales—just thoughtful transcripts of the briefest kind. Proverbs, without doubt, are the words of both scholars and peasants. They share a literary landscape without envy—no awards crown the authors, no royalties are dispersed. They don't take effort to read. They are not riddles or cagey games, but do require an "aha" moment.

Also, proverbs, in all languages and over the centuries, are quips that speak of our human nature. They are tonics against flabby language. They offer an immediate response, in part, because of their visual nature—that is, once the proverb is absorbed it is rendered in the mind as a picture. I'm thinking of the bumper sticker I came upon that read, "Dear Lord, let me be the person my dog thinks I am." Clever, beautifully phrased, and with truth in it—that the judgment of our worth might come from a chihuahua. Not church. Not temple. Not mosque. This could be the proper mantra to follow religiously.

I read this wisdom on a rust-pimpled bumper, and as I strode up the street I had the desire to hug the first leashed pooch that came into view. It affected me. It made me agree with it. I smiled at the notion of trying to live up to the dog's wagging tail.

I have written fourteen poetry collections, many of which contain poems built as narratives with a beginning, middle, and end. Here, in these pages, I brave something new: proverbs that cut to the chase, proverbs that speak of our times—crazy as they are, dangerous as they are, comical as they are. My proverbs, like my narrative poems, are not heady but absorbable as aspirin. So now I'm a doctor? You just read a few of these and you're all better?

Maybe.

But there is no maybe in my reliance upon the everyday—observations on love, home, family, street-life, street thugs, our cynical view of government, deceit in love, food, old age, mortality—in short, human affairs. The sentiments are not new, though the situations apply themselves to the present. I don't expect to pass myself off as a wise sage, though I would be ashamed to be called a wisenheimer. Some of the proverbs are outrageously comical, as the title of this book indicates. And some, the reader will see, play at the edge of the politically incorrect, though none is as offensive as some rap or the nastiest politicians.

Finally, you can begin at the end, the middle, or the first page. These proverbs may at times be bumper-sticker comical; yet, they are literary. They require the gamesmanship all readers dispense when reading: a pleasurable buy-in. And it doesn't hurt to know that these are original and not the stuff of translation or outright borrowing. Like speed-dating, if you don't like one, then you can move to another.

THE PROVERBS

One mosquito
Ruins your sleep
One pesky coworker
Ruins the day

So rough, so angry
Came into the world
With hands balled
Into fists

A good word
For the bad dude
But never a bad word
For the good dude

Two wives
Three children
Four houses
Five jobs
Six cats
Seven cars
What you call a full life

A backbone
Is more useful
Than a wishbone

A protruding chin
Gets there first

The bike built
With stolen parts
Never rides straight

Snowman in sunlight
Knows when to give up

If your only tool
Is a hammer
Everything gets pounded

Looks so poor
Even the flies stay away

The mouth is full of flattery and lies
And to think that that
Is where we kiss

A flower grows
Even among litter

A half-bottle of wine
Produces a good story
The whole bottle a saga

Burger patties on the grill
Hissing at customers

Weekly deductions
From your paycheck
Government thievery

Poker face is best
If you win the lottery

Liquor store dings
When you enter
All eyes on you

Friends cash out
When you're broke

Rocks rolling down a mountain
The gods throwing down
The little people

Imagination
Far greater than fact

Learned to tie a tie
Now with a job
He hangs by a thread

Autumn begins
When the first apple falls

Gossip
An invisible grasshopper
That jumps from yard to yard

A martyr's halo
Is sometimes a noose

Want to know what he's like
Let him steal
And see how he spends

After a fever breaks
The best sleep ever

Three teenage boys
In the living room
Something's going to break

Roughly cut bread
Rough hand behind the knife

Mother cat licks
Her newborn's wounds
Before they even happen

The middle son
Takes the beating

Giving up your seat
On a crowded bus
Makes for a happier ride

Loan him twenty
Next week it's fifty

The poetry slam starts
At 7:00 p.m.
Ends when you turn twenty-five

Pushing a stroller at fifteen
Sentence without parole

Love lightens your step
Hate weighs you down
In heavy boots

Rattle ice in a cup
To make more soda

Day laborers
On the corner
Know about patience

A wasp in a Coke bottle
Sugar junkie

The broom
Knows a thing or two
About dirt

The child refused to grow up
Yet died at ninety

Easier for the young
To leave home
Than to return

      Mop dirtier than the floor
      Think of a politician in action

A million dollar lottery winner
Moves away
Without telling his adult children

      If you go into the store
      You'll buy

Auntie's poodle meets
The curly wig on the bedroom floor
Touches it softly with a paw

      Bars on the front window
      But the back door is wide open

The yard sale
On a yellow lawn
A museum of the poor

The largest body of water
A tear after the breakup

What young lovers
Bring to marriage
Their bodies

A good joke
But not over and over

You polish your car
Bright as a dime
But one bird ruins it

Though filthy rich
He won't even share a smile

The rivulet of melted snow
Joins the river
That flows to the sea

From a distance
Problems seem easy

Two bald men
Fighting over a dropped comb
That's what we call silly

Free concert
Unruly crowd boos

Get a job
Get a house
Then hang with friends

Leaf blower
Just when you begin your nap

The dog's tongue is pink at birth
At death
Purple from use

        Even in the confessional
        The priest hears lies

His belly shakes
When he laughs
That's your Buddha boyfriend

        The hotdog looks
        The same on either end

At every intersection
At every red light
Cameras looking at you

        Ambulance siren
        Trouble going the other way

Want to marry
An older divorced guy
Spend a day with his three kids

The cat watches
The cook's every move

Don't worry
If you're stung by lost love
The sea is filled with other jellyfish

Let children suffer a little
And they'll grow up right

The loud, hotheaded fool
Cool him off with a soda
In the shade

The gangster steals flowers
For his best friend's funeral

The second
The police cruiser passes
You feel better

At a hole-in-the-wall takeout
Flies cut in line

A spoonful of bitter medicine
Is better than a shovel
Of graveyard dirt

The bail bondsman
Welcomes trouble

A spiteful tongue
Is sharper
Than a knife

DMV
Hell without the fire

Six foot six, 210
Sucking his thumb
Because of a paper cut

If it's half off
Not worth stealing

Baby teething
On a pickle
Grows up sour

If you own a pickup truck
Everyone calls

Liars must remember
The place and time
Of their lies

The public library
Is a new kind of church

Bigger concern
Than the world's problems
The thorn in your pinkie

By doing nothing
You remain blameless

Quiet
Like the moment
The thieves roll from the house

The window washer's spit
Never reaches the street

If you're carrying
A ring of keys
You're not the boss

If you watch the soup cook
It'll take longer

Books at your bedside
But the mosquito gets
All your attention

After a death
Paperwork

Your car window smashed
When you get back
Too late to look around

The preacher's son
Is righteously in jail

Rips off a bicycle
To replace his own
That got ripped off

Braces straightened her teeth
But she never straightened out

What goes around
Comes around
Here it comes again

Gum on the sidewalk
The devil's spit

A house fire
Is worse than a thief
For it takes everything

The roofer gets up
Before the rooster

If someone messes you over
Forgive him
But don't forget him

The loud, foul-talking teenager
Had a bad case of death

Reading his tattoos
Like reading a comic book
So many pictures

Car wreck on the corner
Everyone runs to see

A penny looking up at you
Take me home
It pleads

The teething baby
Has every reason to cry

The protestors
For a black cause
Were white

A flyweight boxer
Swift as an electric fan

A casket bought
On layaway
No hope for the teenage son

High school motto
Run like you stole something

Stubborn
Even dying
Keeps his eyes open

On a lined face
Tears know where to travel

Dirty carpet
Always at the entrance
Of the house

Under a scab of hurt love
A very tender spot

Thunderbolt
Like a chrome bumper
Falling from the sky

Rotate your hamburger
See where to begin

Five aunties
In the kitchen
Family recipes for the ages

If you all think the same
No one's doing any thinking

After the break-in
Up to a month
Before the full tally

How does a blind man
Choose his sunglasses?

Too much
Not enough
A fine balance

False teeth
A perpetual smile

If you need a scaffold
To reach your enemy
Forget it

If you succeed
The politicians show up

Man took up
The dog's habit of barking
At people

Heavy jowls
Heavy life

Rolls up a newspaper
To kill a fly
Ends up reading the headlines

With each lick
An ice cream loses its dome

If you can roll
Like a wheel
You're still young

His mouth
A garbage can spilling its guts

At the surface
Of the pond
Koi smack kisses

No more sharing
When your best friend dies

Last stand
For the nearly bald
The hair around the ears

What happens at home
Happens throughout the city

A small plate
Big buffet
Build upwards

A line of ants
Brings home the harvest

Baby looking down
At her first tottering steps
Another happy day

What's yours is yours
Once you pay it off

The lid lifted
From a pot of boiling beans
Angry relatives looking at you

Financial aid application
Harder than college

In France
If the snail doesn't hurry up
It becomes dinner

He was cute until he opened
His mouth

Babies creep
Later they stand up
And ask for the car keys

Don't sign
If you don't have the money

A chicken avoids
A pillow stuffed with feathers
Could be her mother inside

If you're paid by the hour
It's never enough

With a hundred legs
The centipede
Never stumbles

She loves you for a while
Perhaps a lifetime

Not all the flowers
On a flowering tree
Become apples

When you sharpen a pencil
The learning begins

So inked up
With tattoos
He resembles a walking bruise

A promise is just air
Until you do what you say

Even without legs
Rumors gallop
Around the block

A snake is a tape measure
In the wild

Six men in orange vests
Around a sewer hole
City workers talking shit

The clogged sink
Like a cat with hairball

If you sit on a couch
Long enough
You'll make an impression

Can by crushed can
A living for the homeless

Six-foot-five linebacker
Shrinks down
To kiss his granny

A mustard sandwich
Is still a sandwich

Comb claws beak feathers neck
Hardly any edible parts
From a chicken

Better no milk
Than spoiled milk

Getting up for a senior
On a crowded bus
A seat for you in the future

Love is not blind
But in very dark sunglasses

After an outdoor barbecue
Friends leave
Flies stick around

If you're dressed poorly
You're treated poorly

A pretty good rapper in life
But killed in a shootout
A legend

After the picnic
The dog licks the paper plates

When God made earth
He made plenty of it
To bury us all

With hoodies up
All teenagers look dangerous

The tall can't help
But look down
On the short

The go-between gets tired
Trotting back and forth

Staple your tie
To your desk
A lifetime of office work

Feed a dog three times a day
Soon you have a hog

A thief stealing
From another thief
Street economics

The poor look for their rent
The rich wait for their rent

Love and jealousy
No surprise if they spit
At each other

Under a hot sun
A mile seems longer

If you think
Of your greatest fear
It will visit you

The fortune cookie
Is never about you

When the parrot
Was shown the fried chicken
He finally quieted down

Fear your grandma
More than the police

Stepmother
Like a snake
When she caught your dad

Got to listen
To be interesting

The cucumber
Envies the hug
The pumpkin gets

A head of gray hair
You've come pretty far

Right from the grill
A chicken wing
Flies into your mouth

    The old have memories
    If they can remember them

Your car going up
On the mechanic's rack
Gonna cost you money

    If you marry young
    Babies every two years

In a family dispute
Listen to each side
But say nothing

    Casual sex
    "Hi" and "Bye"

Six-pack abs
For the young dudes
Keg for old men

Famous today
Remembered tomorrow

Not a good sign
After they kissed
She wiped her lips

First time cook
Start by boiling water

Bronze statue of a general
Pigeons on his head
Shows a higher status

A flower with one petal
Is still a flower

At birth
Babies look older
Than the old

A shirt on a coat hanger
Better posture than yours

Electric car
Like you
Slow at the start

Without passports
Clouds go where they please

Landline phones
Old folks pick up
On the third ring

Fast food
Slow to burn off

A loud fool skips old age
And at eighteen
Goes right into the grave

Sand doesn't need a straw
To drink its fill

In love
Men go into details
Women go shopping

Juggling two girlfriends
Pretty pies in the air

A Spanish class
Filled with Chinese
The future of things

Polite
A biscuit takes off its hat

Light thinking
When God hands out
The gifts

Voyeur moon looks
In every open window

Like eating a lemon
That's how sour
She is

A missed boat
Sometimes sinks

Brussels sprouts
A cruel veggie
That makes kids bawl

The ukulele
Baby sister of the guitar

Big words
Like talking
Wearing a retainer

Looking to get ahead
Cut in line

Daylight fights darkness
In the end it's a draw
They call it dusk

A menu with pictures
Don't eat there

With lottery tickets
You scratch an itch
To win a million

The rag was once
A new shirt

A pinch of salt
In a pan of boiling weeds
Hobo soup

Scratch your itch
But not in public

There are other fish
In the sea
But some are sharks

If it's illegal
You'll find buyers

In a strong wind
The bras on the clothesline
Fulfill their promise

If kale is good for you
You eat it

Photos embedded
On gravestones
They're looking at you

Too friendly
Be careful

Eyes follow you
Not when you come in
But when you leave

If you listen
You'll learn sooner

Hippo husband
In the bathtub
Water up to his eyes

Asking a lot of questions
You seem smart

Like people
The faces of tortillas
Are never the same

The class clown
Making them smile in prison

In old age
The stallion slows
To a donkey pace

Nice parents
Nice kids

A newspaper
Flying toward your lawn
Disasters in readable print

Candles flicker
Even when lit for a saint

The slot machines
Every one of their arms
Going through your pockets

Parents choose
The street you go down

Early winter
The cat sleeps
On the hood of a warm car

I'll build the house
You do the curtains

Expensive guitar
But he can only play three chords
And badly

Bald tires
Teach your car to crawl

If the doctor comes in
With another doctor
Bad news

Hunger is a beast
Your ribs its cage

Name of the restaurant
At the corner of Lenin and Stalin
Meatballs for the People

There's not a neck
A vampire doesn't like

Second marriages
Both driving high-mileage imports
On a domestic road

A jury of peers
None of them liking you

The mouth makes the promise
But the rest of the body
Has to deliver

Don't hide
In a stolen car

Customer can't do the math
One kind of people says
Cheat him

A belt whipping
Stings into adulthood

After high school
The bully pushes
A wheelbarrow around

In an ESL class
Parrot-talk at first

Fear a ghost floating
Into the bedroom
Where you and his wife sleep

For a nail
The hammer is the final judge

The weakling everyone beat up
In middle school
Survives them all

From eye to hand to canvas
An artist at work

The best fun
A five-year-old
With spoon and sand

Bad breath
Sours a romance

The rich and the poor
Earn from each other
But the rich more

The same value
On either side of a coin

A crying baby
Is different
From a crying teenager

Giving an unexpected gift
Lightens your steps

The glow of a cigarette
On a dark street
A dead giveaway

You can't understand it
Ugly fart with a beautiful lady

Barred windows on a house
Poor parents of six
Can't escape

Rain after a long summer
The grass perks up

The stray dog
Dead near freeway entrance
Went as far as he could go

A frying egg sings
But bacon sings louder

With fisherman in a hurry
Water in the bucket
Rolls like a troubled sea

First in your family in college
Not the last

Little sister
Taller than you
Still looks up to you

    The apple hangs on
    Until wind slaps its face

When a new law is made
An even newer law is made
To get out of it

    The mouth may talk back
    But the body takes the beating

At the city dump
The crows can afford
To be picky

    The highest culinary honor
    Order of the Bacon

Slice of cold pizza
From the fridge
A college student's breakfast

The day after the wedding
The laundry

More sailors drown
In pints of beer
Than they do at sea

An abandoned wheelchair
Possibly a miracle

The marriage vows
Seem easy enough
Until you get home

Car payments
Last longer than the car

Kissing Hello
Kissing Goodbye
Two different stories

A small house
May be just big enough

Born rich
But you end up poor
Better the other way around

Monday was like last Monday
With six days difference

Got to beat
Oil and vinegar
To make them friends

A toe poking through a sock
Just looking around

Grandpa a mechanic
Son a developer
Grandson a couch potato

A startup
An idea with no money

Eat little
Drink a lot
Sleep as you please

Grease finds
The silk blouse

If you hunt with a puppy
You come home
With a squeaky toy

God helps you
And you get the credit

A long weekend starts
By thinking about it
On Thursday

Loud trash talk
But can't back it up

For happiness
In adulthood
Stay away from family

If the salsa is too hot
No flavor

At the bottom
Of a pot of boiling soup
The meatballs are hiding

Stolen goods
Drop big time in value

So sweet
In a bitter world
That's my little girl

Pillow talk
Beautiful nonsense

Meal so delicious
You corner the frijoles
With last bit of tortilla

The phone rings
When you sit down to eat

Even at a party
The dentist can't help
But look at teeth

Manicured fingernails
The rest of her not so nice

Dollar bills stink
From passing through
Sweaty hands

A thong bikini
The floss of a lifetime

To the merchant
Credit cards are OK
But cash is better

A dead son
Shadows his mother daily

A daughter
On the father's shoulder
Great view of the future

Your thumb
The taste of babyhood

The bike before the flat
Was carrying you
Now you carry it

Six beers
Sorrow and a full confession

On Monday
You're already thinking
Of Friday

Lightning
A terrifying strobe

For the widow
The worst gardener
Is better than no gardener

OK to be nice
While arguing

Before you get off
The bus
Feel for your wallet

Climate change
Summer now part of autumn

No talent
Dye your hair blue
For attention

In his spare time
The devil beats his children

Platform shoes
So dangerously high
She could see next week

Naked
You have nothing to lose

Two drunks share
A single bottle
Each counting the gulps

The spiteful mouth
A cave with chisels

The toucan
Every color in a box
Of crayons

A fat lie today
Grows fatter by tomorrow

The bones
Of scrap iron
Material for the sculptor

No one bothers
The ratty ass car

Smoke
Then fire
Then smoke again

One crime
Creates three jobs

The best time
For lovemaking
When the children are not yet born

Royalty don't make names
But inherit them

Helping your friend
Find a boyfriend
You find one yourself

Poor soil
Produces the best weeds

If he has more
Than five credit cards
He's in serious debt

A lazy walker
A lazy soul

Think big
But please keep quiet
About it

The best facelift
A smile

My buddy
Is like a vest
That's how close

Even the sweetest cat
Has fangs

Little thieves
Start by stealing
From the fridge

If you marry young
You've got a long time to go

Upright all day
Your worst human smells
Drain to your feet

She rolled like an ocean
When I lay on top

Speed reading
The summary
On the back cover

Stone soup
Broken teeth

In a lifetime
Only two sets of teeth
But plenty of smiles

A vacuum cleaner
Knows all the dirt

The final side dish
The bill on
A black plastic plate

A tear on the face
Will run its course

A car salesman
Will drive you
To the poor house

Bargains
Get you into debt

Can't smell
The landscape
In a landscape painting

Sugary cereal
Jittery fuel for kids

Two losers
Scoreless
At the end of their lives

Nonprofits
Shouldn't beg

Too late
To speak up
When the judge raps his gavel

The best relatives
Live three time zones away

The latest fashion
Wears out quicker
Than the fabric

If you plant a garden
Get ready to weed

If you beat a child
Of your own flesh
You beat yourself

Twin babies
Blinking at the same time

Sleeping infant
Parents tiptoeing
Around the house

Nothing to do
Keeps you busy

At trial
The thief calls another thief
His expert witness

Smart phone
Dumb conversation

Want to get rid
Of a pest
Loan him money

You become corrupt
In increments

A first grader
With a backpack
Heavier than him

OK if the spilled milk
Is expired milk

Even in rain
The ants push on
With their cargo

Ugly pot
Beautiful soup

If you eat too much
You're digging your grave
With your teeth

If you postpone long enough
You forget

Newborn twins
The first one out
Is ahead of the game

Sour grapes
Eatable with a little sugar

In love with his baritone voice
The politician believes
What he says

Bald tires on a stolen car
Leave no tracks

Leaderless
Cockroaches scatter
When the cellar light goes on

Shy dog
Skinny dog

If a pessimist expects nothing
More of nothing
Is on its way

Can't hide a sin
By wearing a coat

Self-imposed hardship
Burger and fries
With no soda

Chip off the old block
Good carpentry

Hyena soup for first course
Everyone's laughing
When the entrée arrives

You can be silent
And still say what you mean

Ignorance of an ignorant law
That's your position
In court

A tattooed neck
Hides the dirt ring

Not enough cream
In the jar
To make you young again

When you inherit money
You inherit enemies

Impossible
Like tying up fog
And shipping it away

Crooked teeth
But otherwise he's straight

Go room-to-room
Turning off lights
Then sleep

Keep it short
If you have something to say

Before a speech
Drink a little water
To slicken your tongue

In prison
They all say they're innocent

Seven days in a week
Like children
All of them a little different

An oil spot under your car
The devil's black tears

Cheating boyfriend
In a rearview mirror
He's getting smaller and smaller

If we're scared
We all come together

The rapper
With his cap turned sideways
Shades an ear

Worry cuts a path
Across every mother's brow

Can't recall a name
Ask brightly
Remember me

If you let a motor mouth talk
He'll run his engine all day

The taste of learning
A licked finger
Turning the page

A retiree with no hobbies
Whittles away his life

Crooked teeth
Otherwise
A straight face

A wagging tail
Now there's real love

The wrong college
For the right reason
Still works out

New to the country
Just smile

Three kids
On one bike
Off to steal two more

Don't use a snake
For a belt

You can start
On either end
Of a hotdog

A convict
Every day he stays home

The doctor
Explained your ailment
Old age

Dyslectic snack
You eat just the peel

Drone delivery
A wife throwing your dirty sock
Across the bedroom

Fatigue
The best sleeping pill

You stop growing
At fifteen
Time for platform shoes

Bald
But look how he shines

Unlike the mouth
The ear has no say
It must listen to everything

If you eat the bagel
The hole will disappear

Better to elect
The incumbent
He's already stolen everything

With the kids grown up
Good time to nap

Three pups
Same mother
All different

No enemies
Usually no friends

Once a bestseller
Now a lecturer
At a state college

You advise yourself
And still do the wrong thing

Nothing
Took the backseat
To something

Love comes in pairs
Not threesomes

Philanthropic giving
Often comes from the salaries
Of the workers who weren't paid

You can possess a sweet tooth
Without a single tooth left

The structure of bread
Is made mainly
Of tiny holes

A clever squirrel
Rolls the apple home

Anger management
Thirteen people sitting in a circle
A tornado about to start

A fanatic
A logical mind gone crazy

Senior citizens' cheap first date
A two-for-one coupon
Doggie bag to take home

Straw burns quickly
Love roars even faster

A hen with a hen brain
Busily fattens herself
For Sunday

The egotist needs a thick neck
To balance his big head

At a round table
No matter where you sit
All are equals

Plant cucumbers
And the weeds appear

If you rob a Guatemalan
You rob his family
Waiting for the monthly money order

For the laborer
Sundown never comes soon

For the billionaire
With seven houses
Where is home

Iron
Rust's favorite flavor

The wrong answer
From a lovely mouth
Convinces the old professor

The taste of ash
The taste of cremation

Start a restaurant
Then convince people
They're hungry

The flipside of a joke
Sarcasm

If you get a flat tire
In a barrio
You risk fate

Don't make a grocery list
While hungry

Carpentry was Jesus's trade
Clergy since His time
Have built on it

Moth
A butterfly without makeup

Springy female pubic hair
Meeting a beard
A convention of sorts

Promise and delivery
At least one mile part

The day before
Thanksgiving
Stop eating

White collar crime
Dirty collar

The tongue
Is not a fist
But it can hurt

Sunglasses
Cool a hot day

The only fly
At the party
Finds your plate

The tomato gave its life
To become ketchup

Hearing aid turned up
Still doesn't like
What you're saying

Fire burned
His friend Straw

New clothes
Old clothes
Gotta mix it up

Crumbs to you
Boulders to the ant

Turning a coconut
In your hands
How do you get in?

A bad relief pitcher
Blames the ball

You've lived a long time
If your clothes
Have come back into style

A pillow understands
The heartbreak

In hell there are fans
But no wall sockets
To plug them in

Don't call it arson
If you burn your own bridges

In one seed
A tree bursting
To get out

Smooth talker
Irons out the argument

It's a real workout
For your jaw
If you use big words

Better to mess up in youth
Than in old age

Quarrel with a friend
She'll bring up
Everything she knows about you

A swift river
Bullies the pebbles along

Sorrow walks slowly
Head down
Hands in pockets

Yes and *No*
Sibling rivalry

Rumor
Like a tornado
Will pick up speed

Food-stained apron
The cook trying everything

When you make a contract
With the devil
Don't use your real name

A tiger cub was born
With his sergeant stripes

Teeth cleaned
By a dental hygienist
Good day to smile

A tarantula
Dracula's hairpiece

The eyes speak first
Then the mouth
Takes over

Consider the big toe
Uncle to the little toes

Application form
At a fast food restaurant
Flies looking over your shoulder

Gentrification creeps
House by house

An owner's car manual
Another kind of Bible
You never open

With yellow hair
Sunshine even at midnight

Going against the grain
Lots of slivers
In your palms

The foundation of a river
The stones below

Minor rock star
Walking on snow
Leaves a brief footprint

If you have five credit cards
You're asking for it

The bigger the city
The more people
You don't have to know

In winter
It takes two to keep warm

Birkenstock sandals
Like lawn furniture
On your feet

Best friends build upon
What each other says

It's easier to argue
For what you believe
Than live by what you believe

Hurling a word of anger
A spear with a blunt point

Carrot sticks
Feed for ponies
And children

God forgives sin
But the law won't

With no backbone
Oatmeal carries you
No farther than midday

A storeowner smiles
When he makes a deal

The happy cultivate roses
For scent and beauty
The bitter for thorns

Stale bread
Toast it

Pet a sleeping cat
Against the grain
He wakes up

Stand far from a breakup
See how it happened

Every day in the news
The same mayhem
But different people

A braying donkey
Speaks his mind

For shade
The ant carries a leaf
Overhead

The cracked plate
Hand dry with tenderness

Surprised to see a friend
At the soup kitchen
Eat with him

With office work
You sweat inside

Gold sneers at silver
Silver looks down on bronze
Bronze sneezes at tin

The prom is one night
But the prom picture is forever

Male nudists
Will happily display
Their shortcomings

If visiting Pinocchio
Don't bring up noses

A wet cat
Dries off
By licking herself

A shallow mind
Doesn't drown

Pit bull
Like My Little Pony
But for gangsters

The lid of a boiling pot
Rains when you lift it

City workers talk
While leaning on their shovels
Overtime they just talk

Water running in the gutter
Is looking for its mother

A young man
Pulling up his pants
One less eyesore

Art doesn't have to speak
To convey its meaning

If you find
Yourself among lions
Roar and throw your tail around

Use both hands
When you offer help

Two turtles looking
At each other
Both slow to make a move

More scent
In a long nose

Front teeth to tear
Back teeth to chew
Tongue to slap it down

A motherless kitten
Will lick a beard

Anger
Burrs and thorns
Trying to attach themselves

Waiting all your life
At the wrong corner

Work is sour
But its purchasing power
Sweet

Twitter in phrases
Write in sentences

In old age
Your turn to listen
To the children

Cracked open
A pomegranate shows us
Jewels

The rich aren't thinking about you

The snail outruns
The procrastinator

A bat hanging upside down
From a tree
A scary fruit

Comfortable life
Conservative life

Tacos
Little meat purses
With lettuce hanging out

The late sun dies
In deer tracks
Filled with rain

Soldiers in step think the same

A person can't be wise
Without listeners

If you don't want much
It's easy to bargain with yourself
For even less

The thief sleeps
In running position

A car with different
Colored fenders
Poor guy's restoration

Smoke envies darkness

Don't go on and on
If you know the answer

The extras
On a major motion picture
Loathe the lead

When husband and wife argue
The china in the cabinet trembles

Chipping away
You find a heart
Inside a stone

Bad luck
Like a dragon's tail
Whips you down the road

Know more than you let on

A terminal disease sprints away
With your bag of hours

You never think about the roof
Until the tornado comes
And gets it

Each eye receives
An equal portion of light

A small electric car
Just a toaster
With wheels

Three days after blooming
The peony throws down
Its sunshine

Costs nothing to kiss

When the winter river recedes
Once again revealing stepping stones
Then you know the way

If Mexican American
Mexican is always first

Enough fleas
In bed
To move the blanket

Always a three-act drama
In the house next door

A non-functioning doorbell
Press to get in
The exclusive club

The turtle is always at home

Perhaps
Is not as doubtful
As it seems

A social climber
Brings his own ladder

With repeated licks
Of his tongue
The dog heals his wounds

With a shallow spoon
You must eat more quickly

If it was free
It went into the drawer
Of forgotten things

I was acquainted with money
But a true friend to poverty

Lies in childhood
Lies in adolescence
Then politics

The audience applauded
That the play was finally over

In a fender bender
Both drivers stand by their lies

Ice
Temporary
Like people we know

The root cause
Of curly hair
Wild thoughts

Looking for street parking
Drive turtle-slow

Can't be pornography
If both hands
Are on the book

Can't explain in words
Use your eyes and hands

Civility went out of fashion
About the time the wide tie disappeared

A girl with long hair
More of the same
Inside her head

Proposing on one knee
A gallant position
On two knees
Plain begging

Hoarded money
A great financial constipation

Don't shake hands
With an alligator
Short arms
Razor teeth

Touch a handrail
Before descending

After a squabble in court
Both parties sulk away
With only the buttons
On their hawked shirts

In old age
One blue sock
One black
Close enough

Selling life insurance
Selling someone short

Newborn
Your first duty
Is breathe and cry
And repeat often

Once you have power
Difficult to let go of it

In the hood
Gangbangers and pastors
Run neck-and-neck
In their recruiting efforts

Bluffing in a game of poker
His eyes move
From side to side
Such a rookie

Rats in the walls
Work on the nightshift

Holes at the knees
Bleach stains on thigh and butt
Designer jeans
$300 a pair

At harvest
A potato comes up for air

A flirtatious wind
Will lift a hem
Above the knee
Sometimes higher

I would give you my life
Dear friend
But I'm using it
At the moment

A banana grows freckles
As it ages

Napkin dropped by a homely man
Looks like litter
Dropped by a beautiful girl
A large white flower

The sombrero
A shady awning

A preacher hollering
Is hollering
For the twenties
In your wallet

In the arms of a wolf
Carefully peel the paws off you
As for the teeth in your neck
Wait for him to breathe

Losing an adult tooth
The start of the end

Platonic love
The boring episode
Between a breakup
And finding new love

A shaved armpit
Carries little scent

Reading the ingredients
On the side of a diet soda
The one you recognize
Water

High school lovers
Under a tree
A remake
Of Adam and Eve

A Guatemalan tamale
Is mostly leaf

You the defendant
The judge
Your ex-father-in-law
Doesn't look good

Dying to have everything
You die with nothing

Difficult as opening
A new jar of olives
That's how it is
To get him to talk

Inspiration
A butterfly on a flower
It's there
Then not there

A full head of hair
Never goes out of fashion

After a while
Your prolonged crying
Like a kettle on the stove
Not listened to

Fender bender
Costs more than the car

Marrying a boy
From high school
Now together in the same class
All your life

Learns to tie
His shoelaces at six
Later lets them drag
For affect

When you're wrong
You get even more pissed off

When you help a friend
You store up a gentle debt
He'll come back
And help you

Marry a skinny man
He could fill out later

The newborn comes out
Not crying
But holding his breath
Already stubborn

In the coin dish
The penny children
Snuggle up to their big daddies
The quarters

After the joke
Her smile comes slowly

No dog in the yard
The cat is king
No cat in the yard
The birds rule

Confetti
Tears of joy in paper form

Pitiful shoes
Shoddy coat
Poor everything
But the smile

Long strides
To grow
Then short steps
To the grave

Moonlight
Enough to steal by

Now light
Now dark
Now light again
You blinking

How you speak
Is how we will know you

The single man
And the single woman
Were happy
Then they met

Shrimp boy
In childhood
Whale man
In adulthood

Heroes are in the next city
Never on our own street

Flies leave
A chicken bone
At the rumor
Of a rack of lamb

Can't spell
Slur your penmanship

A squirt gun
In a kid's hand
The cops bring out
Their armor

If a bearded goat
Knew a few more sounds
He would preach
From the pulpit

Crying baby
Almost like a monster

The politician
Stains on his tie
Crumbs on his lap
Dough in his pocket

Friends made quickly
Go away quickly

The bottle
With a slender neck
And fat waist
Some people are like that

The trumpet hanging
In the pawn shop
Waits for the rest of the band
To show up

Like trusty dogs
Your old shoes

Choir member
If you forget the words
Just make your jaw
Go up and down

Cruel to be happy
Around sad people

Rich family
Poor family
For the dog
No matter

A bachelor cries
Not over love
But for the horse
That comes in third

A frown does more damage
Than the sun

Boys in a herd
Young men in pairs
Oldster alone
With his walker

Diamonds may be forever
Death just a little longer

Old goats playing chess
In the park
Each pulling on his beard
In thought

His beard
A hedge
His tongue
A talking bird

Rudimentary place setting
The meat goes on the plate

Arms
Long enough
To wrap around
Big love

Deep love
Then hatred sometimes

The day laborer
At the corner
Does more waiting
Than work

Twist your guts
Into a heart
When you say
I love you

Taught him to box
Now he's beating you up

More money withdrawn
From the ATM
Than going in
This is how you get poor

With swinging dreadlocks
The back takes the whipping

Left foot
Right foot
Each racing to stay
In the lead

In bed
Lovers
Not in bed
Spouses

Virtue takes the fun
Out of life

Prairie wheat
In wind
The soothing hush
Of acres

Two loudmouths
The start of political parties

The woodpecker knocks
And knocks
Then calls the hole
Home

Church ladies
With their hats
A line of beautiful hens
Going up the steps

If it's free drinks
You drink freely

If the tree
Doesn't bear in three years
It's kindling for the fireplace
The fourth year

The small cloud
Gave all the rain

Time is slow
In childhood
A clock gone crazy
In old age

Panties on a clothesline
In wind they dance like flowers

Forgive most
Forget none

When you're cheated
Think of it as checks and balances

The skunk gets his way

Firecracker
That's how the hothead explodes

Little brother trots
In your shadow

Some need some things
And some need everything

Curly hair
Spring in her steps

Fingers
The first fork

Soap and a shower
You're new again

Love can go around corners

Compassion for living creatures
Except bedbugs

Even panhandlers
Deserve a day off

If you hang with Frankenstein
You'll walk like Frankenstein

An echo knows infinite languages

Time cures smoked hams
And broken hearts

A grassy bank sucks appreciatively
From a slow-flowing river

An idea is not touchable
Until fabricated

Can't talk straight with a snake

Hotdogs three days
Steak on the fourth

Money and I once shook hands
Then we said our goodbyes

Good looks add to the resume

Puts on his T-shirt backwards
That's how he does things

Crows around road kill
Pallbearers from the bird world

Feasting on illusion
You go hungry

Locusts can kick start a famine

Uninvited
But still goes

Steals seeds
Under his fingernails

It's a brave bird
Who chirps in a sleeping cat's ear

A wobbly pup
Stirs our hearts

Flies have replacements

For better or worse
No retreat in marriage

Smoke goes where the wind tells it

Special child
Hug her even more

Bull in a china shop
Just browsing

Eightieth birthday party
Impossible to blow out the candles

To get it done
Go to bed early

The river never tires of running

In the hunt
Cats work alone

Army ants have their marching orders

The rooster
Needs no winding

Wets his lips
Before a dry speech

If the new boyfriend talks a lot
He'll lie a lot

Paid too much for a car
Just keep it longer

Money goes to the wrong people

Through a head of hair
The comb ploughs for lint

A ladle
The mother of all spoons

Ivy grows only so far

Smoke bumps against brick
As it climbs the chimney

A fox can explain
The feathers around his mouth

At the dollar store
OK to pay in pennies

Fleas make the lion roar

At a formal dinner
Don't tuck in your jacket

Only long-sleeve shirts
For Mr. Skinny Arms

Every tree invites the wind

Double chin
Swallows twice

An open coffin
Can keep the conversation going

When the leaves fall
The naked tree shivers

Habit is unbendable

House in foreclosure
Rats move in

Darkness
Makes the lamp bright

There are no old flies

Ladders
The envy of stepstools

A river flows south
Taking with it logs and alligators

In hot weather
Anger like red ants

Not much income in honesty

Big feet in a small shoe
The toes squished all in a row

The shape of her eyes
Bitter almonds

No immediate cure for hate

Your shadow
Mimics your every move

A famished scarecrow
That was how skinny the poet was

A running back
Runs for his paycheck

Don't shake hands with a crab

Running downhill
Even the oldsters are swift

Walking uphill
Like knee-deep mud

Weeds are not picky

A handgun
Is never aimless

The nonprofit's dishonest hand
Went through charity's coat pockets

A bag of potato chips
But not at every meal

Stick around if you start a fire

Dead
The trout loses its rainbow

Not all rivers
Reach the sea

A burden gives purpose

You want to pull her hair
To discover where her wits are

Spanish speakers
Attract other Spanish speakers

Flowers open their mouths
When the sprinklers come on

Marriage is a beginning and an end

Even the rocker falls asleep
Hearing a lullaby

The dandelion
Scatters itself

A sliver gets all the attention

A bird walks
When he feels like it

Money or love
Occasionally you have to choose

Surprised
The mouth drops open

A short cut takes longer

Red eyes
Either from drink or studying

Headlights out of alignment
That's how he sees things

Athletes run in the family

Not much faith
When you're hungry

Text and drive
Why not a cheeseburger as well

    Junior high dropouts
    Stunted little trees

The bank teller knows your worth

    The weather changes
    When you wear a straw hat

Rainy day spending
Begins soon after the first sprinkles

    Every flower has her day

A starving rat
Will eat its whiskers

Six daughters
Quiet father in the background

Can't be rap
If *bitch* ain't hollered

A drum takes the beating

The running back
Only looks forward

The fool peels back a scab
Just to see

Time never plays dead

Mother duck and ducklings
An armada in late spring

Pineapple
Fruit with the most exotic hairdo

Two pints
Buys a poet

A thief in every nonprofit

A beaten child
Beats her dolls

With no sleeves or collar
Consider the vest a poor man's shirt

Yes is friendlier than *No*

Open a door for others
And others will be open to you

A crab bites like a clothespin
And hangs on

A dog using the can opener
An unforeseen evolution

A fence can't keep flies out

Rotten teeth
Rotten breath behind them

At your high school reunion
Classmates as old as the teachers

Ducks think nothing of rain

Whisper into a gossip's ear
And her eyes get big

Bad luck if you're fired
Good luck for your replacement

Sleep heals a cold

A cashier
Touches more money than most

A mushroom in the wild
A game of chance

Coffee makes you smarter

The fly does its best
To clean up after you

A yard sale
Another person's lousy purchases

Living within your means
Means you're sleeping in a doorway

Takes two to run a house

A chubby cheerleader
Like throwing a piano in the air

Always some sense
In nonsense

Every bush hides a rabbit

The mural on a restaurant wall
Worse than the food

Sitting down
You can't fall too far

A tortoise resides in his future coffin

      Curse the rain
      In winter
      Beg for it
      In summer

Hit a tall guy
He sways like a tree
Hit a squat guy
He moves one inch
Like a boulder

      A sweet tooth rots quickly

Crib
Bunk
Sleeping bag
Marriage bed
Coffin with a hollow ring
Comfy places in the right order

Be brave when no one is looking

Leaf blower
Your wife
When she hears
About the girlfriend

Thirteen houses
In a month
The thief pleads
A bad habit
Not a crime

Even the obese get hungry

Small talk
Weather
Children and wife
Job
Plans for a vacation
Then the pitch

A high school textbook
Is like a brick
In your backpack
Line it up with others
And you build on them

Four is fine dining
Seven a buffet
Nine a party
Eleven a fundraiser
Thirteen famine relief

The safest way home
Where everyone's walking

A hungry bear has no patience

An outhouse door
Flapping open
Again and again
That's him cussing

Grand Opening
Next to Clearance Sale
Across from Lost Our Lease
And in view of Going out of Business
Commerce for the hopeful

For six blocks
Snow clings
To the hood of a car
Then like fingers
Loses its grip

In the rearview mirror
Your business rivals on your tail

Pit bull on a leash
Holds back his barking owner

Boots trudging on snow
The sound of the ice man chewing

BIOGRAPHICAL NOTE

Gary Soto is author of more than thirty-five books for young readers and adults. His popular titles include *Baseball in April, Buried Onions, New and Selected Poems, Living Up the Street, A Summer Life* and *Too Many Tamales.* His poem "Oranges" is the most anthologized poem in contemporary literature. His work has sold nearly five million copies. The Gary Soto Literary Museum is located at Fresno City College, where he began to write poetry in spring 1972. He lives in Berkeley, California.

CPSIA information can be obtained
at www.ICGtesting.com
Printed in the USA
BVOW09s2131080817
491534BV00002B/2/P